Echoes From Within

Soyar Kaping Ruivah

BookLeaf Publishing
India | USA | UK

Presentation by *BookLeaf Publishing*

Web: www.bookleafpub.com

E-mail: info@bookleafpub.com

ISBN: 9789360943226

First edition 2024

This book is lovingly dedicated to the memory of my dear grandmother, Mahala Kaping. Her wisdom, love, and gentle spirit continue to inspire me every day. Though she may no longer be with us, her presence lives on in the pages of this book and in the depths of my heart.

ACKNOWLEDGEMENT

My deepest gratitude goes to my family for their unwavering love, unwavering support, and unwavering encouragement. They have been my steadfast anchor throughout this journey, providing me with the strength and motivation to keep going.
I extend a heartfelt thank you to Bookleaf Publishing for not only believing in me but also for playing a pivotal role in making my dream a reality. Your support and guidance have been invaluable, and I am truly grateful for the opportunity to work with such a dedicated team.
To all my friends, I am immensely thankful for your unwavering support and encouragement. Your belief in me has been a source of inspiration and motivation.
Above all, I offer my deepest gratitude to the Almighty for blessing me with the opportunity to pursue my passion and for guiding me every step of the way.

PREFACE

Welcome, dear reader, to "Echoes From Within." As you hold this collection of poetry in your hands, I invite you to embark on a journey of introspection, emotion, and discovery. These poems are more than just words on a page—they are echoes of the soul, reflections of the human experience in all its complexity and beauty. Each verse is a testament to the power of language to capture the fleeting moments of longing, love, childhood innocence, nostalgia, loss, and adventure that shape our lives.

For me, writing poetry has always been a deeply personal and cathartic experience. It is a way to make sense of the world around me, to explore the depths of my own heart, and to connect with others on a level that transcends words alone. In "Echoes From Within," I have poured my heart and soul into each poem, drawing inspiration from the people, places, and moments that have touched me deeply throughout my life.

I believe that poetry has the power to heal, to inspire, and to remind us of our shared humanity. It is my hope that as you read these poems, you will find moments of solace, moments of recognition, and moments of

connection with your own innermost thoughts and emotions.
So, dear reader, I invite you to journey with me through the pages of "Echoes From Within." May these whispered words resonate in your heart, stir your soul, and remind you of the beauty and fragility of the human experience.

With love and gratitude,
Soyar Kaping Ruivah

Love's Guiding Light: A Tribute to Grandmother

In the heart of our family, a guiding light, A grandmother's love, pure and bright. With tender care and gentle grace, She shaped our lives, in her embrace.

She named me with joy and pride, A bond of love, never to hide. In her grocery store, I learned to stand, Amongst shelves stacked with dreams, so grand.

With wisdom beyond her years, she'd impart, The art of business, from her heart. In every lesson, her love would shine, Guiding me through life's design.

She prayed and sang hymns, day and night, A beacon of faith, in the darkest plight. Her voice, a melody of peace, As she found solace, in God's grace.

And when her time on earth was through, She left us with memories, forever true. Peacefully, she slipped away, Leaving behind a legacy to stay.

In the quiet moments after her gentle farewell, we searched her belongings, each one to unveil. And in her wardrobe, tucked away with care, An envelope awaited secrets share.

Inside, a photograph of me lay, Beside her pension book, in a quiet display. She kept my teenage smile within her. How did I know she carried it so secretly?

Through the years, she held onto memories, of cherished moments, like leaves on trees. Her love, a silent whisper in every glance, a testament to our enduring dance.

Though she's journeyed beyond this earthly shore, Her love remains, forevermore. In every heartbeat, in every sigh, Her love sings, an eternal lullaby.

"Untold Depths of Innocent Flames"

In childhood's innocence, they roamed as
friends, Growing slowly, as love's silent
blends. Though words unsaid, their
action spoke clear, A love language
whispered, year after year.

In the girl's house, most nights they'd stay,
caring for each other in a silent display.
As hometown boys sang love songs by the fire's
glow, Her ears caught his voice,
amidst the soft flow.

No regular power, just candlelight's dance,
Guiding his steps in their nightly romance.
She'd keep the candle burning, a sign so
bright, That she waited awake, in the soft
candlelight.

Through the window, he'd see the flames gentle flicker, A silent promise, in the dark, getting flicker. He'd sing her a goodnight, in a melody pure, A secret shared, a love that would endure.

As they grew older, paths led them astray. Separated by distance, yet in memory they'd stay. Now married to others, their love finds its place, But echoes of their past, no time can erase.

Innocent, pure, and true, their love's refrain, In childhood's embrace, it forever will remain. Though life's journey took them far and wide, Their love, like a candle, never dims nor hides.

"The Streets of Awontang: Where Memories and Dreams Collide"

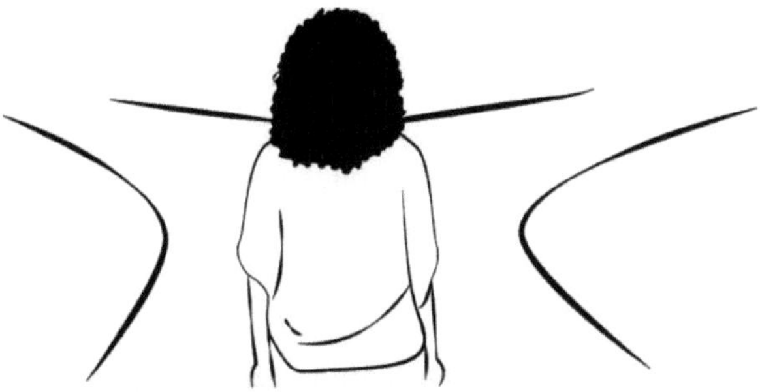

Upon the Awontang's streets, where memories dwell,
Streets whisper tales of each soul's stride.
To birdsong's tune and roosters' call,
Awake to the dawn, where dreams enthrall.

With each morning breeze, a symphony plays,
As shopkeepers greet with the dawn's first rays.
Sweeping the streets, their daily chore,
In Awontang's heart, memories soar.

In the tapestry of streets, lives intertwine,
Awontang's embrace, an eternal shrine.
To the distant pond, where laughter gleams,
Where every maiden's hope beams.

In the workshop's hum, stories intertwine,
As vehicles mend, a testament to time.
Farmers tread paths to their rice fields wide,
Students march forth, with knowledge as their guide.

In Awontang's alleys, love's secrets confide,
Where every corner holds a story inside.
With each passing night, tales unfurl,
In the heart of Awontang, love's eternal swirl.

In times of need, the youth unite,
Working hand in hand, with hearts alight.
Shouldering burdens, with hope aglow,
Together they strive, through highs and lows.

Oh, may the streets of Awontang forever glow,
Guiding the youth as they learn and grow.
May their stories be many, their journeys bold,
In the heart of Awontang, may their futures unfold.

So let the birds sing and the roosters crow,
As the youth of Awontang continue to sow.
With each sunrise, a promise anew,
In Awontang's streets, may dreams come true.

Questioning Life's Tapestry

In the moon's gently glow, a solemn plea,
Questions arise, seeking answers free.
Why does love's journey unfold, yet flee,
Leaving souls adrift, in uncertainty's sea?

From cradle to twilight, destiny's hand,
Some blessed with plenty, others
Withstand. Why does disparity persist,
across the land, Leaving hearts to ponder,
fate's demand?

Why do we labor, with hearts so true, In
pursuit of dreams, old and new? Why does
the weight of toil, our spirits imbue, As we
strive for purpose, in all we pursue?

And when rejection's shadow darkens our
door, Why do we rise, and yearn for more?
Why does unemployment strike, to our core,
As we seek our place, forevermore?

In the tapestry of life, question's weave,
Guiding us through what we believe. In the
pursuit of truth, we cleave, To the hope
that answers, we'll receive.

A Love Once Shared, Remembered Forever

In a tiny town, a tale was spun, Of love's sweet bloom beneath the sun. A couple dear, the talk of the land, Their love story, forever renowned.

As time tiptoed by, their paths did part, Yet memories lingered, etched in the heart. Years later, as I met him anew, Curiosity sparked, the story grew.

"Do you still remember her?" I dared to ask, After thirty years, an impossible task? To my surprise, he softly replied. "I remember those days, with love and pride."

A love once shared, still cherished today,
In the depths of his heart, it found a way.
He dreamed of a film, their love to portray,
To sit by her side, and relive each day.

I shared his wish with a smile and a sigh,
Her reaction, a mix of shock and high.
Miles apart, yet their bond remained
strong. Forgiveness found, amidst all the
wrong.

But fate, in its cruel and relentless stride,
Brought news of his return, no longer
alive. She mourned the loss, of a love once
so true, Their story now etched in the sky's
deepest blue.

For love knows no bounds, in life or in
death, It lingers forever, in each whispered
breath. Though time may keep them worlds
apart, A love once shared remains etched
In the heart.

Tin Roof Melodies

Beneath the tin roof's gentle croon,
Where whispers of rain play their tune.
As raindrops dance in rhythmic rhyme,
I drift to sleep in tranquil time.

Wrapped snugly in my cozy bed,
With blankets soft, dreams are fed.
I listen to the falling rain's tale,
A soothing melody, never frail.

With pillow plush beneath my head,
I lay, worries quietly shed.
In dreams, I wander softly deep,
As rain's sweet lullaby I keep.

Each droplet's murmur, soft and light,
Guides me through the tranquil night.
So let the rain continue to pour,
For in its soothing rhythm, I soar.

Echoes of Love's Journey

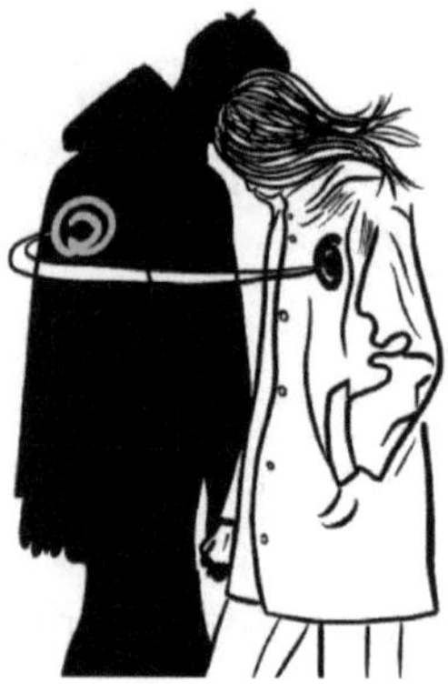

One fine afternoon, where memories gleam,
He found me, in white, like a whispered dream.
An angel's smile, wavy hair's serene,
His heart stirred, love's tender unseen.

Through time's gentle passage, I failed to
perceive,
His silent affection, like a hidden weave.
Yet as closeness grew, our souls did cleave,
Every day, in love's dance, we would believe.

Butterflies danced within our souls' embrace,
His touch, a celestial journey's grace.
"I am the best," his words would trace,
Yet destiny's hand, did we ever face.

One call away, his promise did ring,
Yet parted, harsh words did sting.
Love's flower once bloomed, a fragile thing,
Now melted away, like snow in spring.

No blame to lay, as time softly unfurls,
For love's delicate bloom, oft withers, as it swirls.

Moon's Silent Solace

In the tranquil hours 'neath your gentle light,
We share our dreams, our fears take flight.
Conversing with you, our silent confidant,
In the quiet of night, our secrets enchant.

Oh, moon, you embrace humanity's plight,
Amidst your beauty, amidst your light.
With each admiring gaze from afar,
You hold us close, like a guiding star.

Through the stillness of the night, we speak,
To your ethereal presence, humble and meek.
You listen, you understand, without a word,
In your tranquil embrace, our voices are heard.

In your luminous glow, we find our release,
A sanctuary for our souls, a moment of peace.
Moon, our secret keeper, guardian of the night,
In your silent embrace, everything feels right.

Social Media's Hidden Realms

Social media, a labyrinth of the mind,
A mirror reflecting what's hidden, undefined.
Like a river, it flows with currents unseen,
Shaping perceptions, molding the screen.

Its depths hold treasures, stories untold,
Yet also harbor shadows, secrets unfold.
Like a whisper in the wind, it spreads its reach,
Connecting souls, yet blurring truth's speech.

It's a canvas for dreams, a stage for the bold,
But also a battleground, where lies are sold.
Like a tapestry woven with threads of light,
It illuminates paths, yet veils insight.

In its depths, we find echoes of our desires,
But also echoes of pain, fueling raging fires.
Like a journey into the unknown, it beckons us
near,
To explore its depths, confront our fears.

So let us dive deeper, with eyes wide open,
Navigate its currents, though treacherous,
unbroken.
For in the labyrinth of social media's embrace,
Lies the power to unite or further the chase.

Spring's Melodic Bloom

Pink petals dancing,
Cherry blossoms in the breeze,
Spring's sweet symphony.

Duet of Contrasts

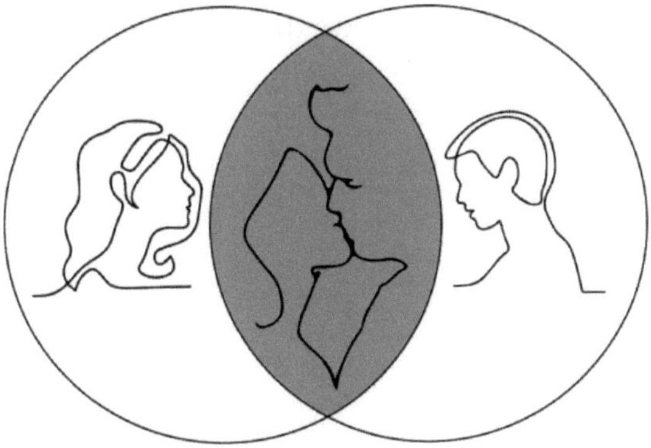

Within the spectrum of differences, we find our tune,
Two souls divergent, yet bound in commune.
He, the quiet whisper, I, the vibrant shout,
In our differences, love finds its route.

Bringing warmth in his gentle embrace,
While I paint smiles with my lively grace.
In the symphony of opposites, we thrive,
His quiet strength, my spirited drive.

Where I speak volumes, he utters with care,
Yet his words, like whispers, reach deep and rare.
For in the silence between his lines,
I find solace, where love intertwines.

In the fabric of quiet and loud,
Our love, a melody, profound and proud.
For in our differences, we discover the key,
To unlock the depths of unity.

Christmas Joy in Ukhrul Town

As November's last week unfolds its grace,
Ukhrul town prepares for Christmas's embrace.
Young and old, from every walk of life,
Anticipate the joy, free from strife.

Songs of Christmas fill the early morn,
With firewood gathered to keep warm.
With holiday approaching, hearts alight,
For Christmas brings a break, a shining light.

Advent sees the streets adorned with care,
Each house and street a festive affair.
Clothes shopping bustling, secondhand treasures found,
Warm garments fill the streets, spreading cheer around.

Locality pride in tree decoration shines bright,
Bringing communities together in festive delight.
Families gather, from distant lands they roam,
To find solace and love within the home.

Christmas feast is rich and keen, a savory delight,
Almost all indulge, from morning to night.
At midnight, church bells ring with joyous sound,
In new warm clothes, the faithful gather 'round.

After a hearty meal, they all gather on the grounds for merriment and games.
Prizes are awarded, and the beloved jaggery is distributed to each and every one.

This beloved treat is most savored at night,
Accompanied by a comforting cup of hot water, providing warmth and solace on the chilly evening.

Youth roam the streets, their spirits high,
Their fashion sense alive, catching every eye.
Singing, joking, beneath the starry sky.

In Ukhrul town, alive with festive cheer,
The season's delight brings everyone near.

A Struggle for Tangkhul Women's Identity

Embedded deep in Tangkhul's ethos, her tale unwinds,
A journey of identity, where paths twist and bind.
Beneath her father's clan's protective shield,
But marriage beckons, a new bond revealed.

Her name echoes her father's lineage, clear and defined,
In school records scripted, her past outlined.
Yet wedded, her loyalty now bends,
To her husband's clan, where tradition extends.

In modern times, bureaucracy's firm grip,
Aadhar cards and passports, a bureaucratic trip.
Navigating the labyrinth of paperwork's chore,
Her identity shifts, seeking something more.

But divorce brings a poignant twist,
No longer his, nor on her father's list.
Caught in a cultural tug-of-war,
Her path uncertain, her identity raw.

Seeking solace in another's fold,
Yearning for stories yet untold.
A culture both enchanting and stern,
Where women's paths face a partial turn.

For men, ties to father's name remain,
While women's roles, under strain, wane.
In tradition's web, choices confound,
Her identity adrift, in a maze profound.

Yet within this tapestry of tradition's decree,
Resides the essence of her legacy.
A yearning for belonging, a quest for grace,
In the heart of Tangkhul, her story finds its
space.

Whispers of Apology: A Farewell Wish

Beneath the night's quiet veil, where stars softly gleam,
I offer my apologies, like a heartfelt stream.
For the pain I've caused, runs deep and true,
Leaving scars that I wish I could undo.

With every tear that falls from your eyes,
My heart shatters anew, under somber skies.
I never meant to hurt you, I swear,
Yet my actions spoke louder than words could bear.

Now as we stand at the crossroads of fate,
I offer you my sincerest of late.
Though gone is gone, and tears may flow,
I wish you healing, wherever you go.

May time be kind, and wounds find peace,
As your broken heart begins to release.
In the tapestry of life, may you find rest,
And know you're cherished, even as we part
best.

So here's my wish, with love untold,
For your journey ahead, may it unfold.
With brighter days and skies above,
Wishing you the best, with heartfelt love.

Realm of What If

If I were the most beautiful woman in the world,
With grace and elegance, my beauty unfurled.
If I were the most beautiful woman in the world,
I'd radiate kindness, my compassion swirled.

If I were a queen, with a crown to wear,
Ruling with wisdom, with dignity rare.
If I were a queen, with a realm to reign,
I'd foster peace and harmony, erasing every pain.

If I were a singer, with a voice to soar,
Serenading the world, forevermore.
If I were a singer, with melodies divine,
I'd touch hearts and souls, in every line.

If I were a billionaire, wealth in my hand,
Uplifting the needy, across every land.
If I were a billionaire, with fortunes to share,
I'd spread hope and joy, beyond compare.

If I were invisible, unseen by all eyes,
Witnessing secrets whispered under moonlit skies.
If I were invisible, with no one to see,
Exploring the world's wonders, wild and free.

If I were the wish maker, granting desires untold,
Sprinkling stardust on dreams, turning them bold.
If I were the wish maker, with magic at hand,
Bringing joy to all hearts, across every land.

If I were the president, with power and might,
Leading with compassion, in the darkest of night.
Striving for justice and equality for all,
Building bridges of unity, standing tall.

But I'm just a commoner, dreaming from afar,
Wishing for a world where all souls shine like stars.
Hoping for happiness to fill every heart's space,
In this dreamer's vision, a brighter world we embrace.

The Inner Conflicts

Within the core of my being, a fire does blaze,
A hunger for more, eager to amaze.
I feel the pull of destiny's call,
Yet lost in a labyrinth, I stall.

Yearning to rise, to stand tall and bright,
On larger stages, bathed in celestial light.
But the road ahead is shrouded in mist,
I long to break free, to cease to exist.

Existing in this realm feels like a plight,
An arrow piercing through eternal night.
Will life remain static, forever enshrined?
Or will I spread my wings, leaving doubt
behind?

Sadness and doubt, they burden my soul,
But a glimmer of hope, it refuses to part.
I ache to soar, to touch the sky,
To see where my aspirations will fly.

Though my wings may be hidden, yet to unfurl,
I'll keep striving forward, through each trial and twirl.
For deep within, I know I'll find,
The fortitude to soar, leaving doubt far behind.

A Poet's Mind

A poet, lost in their labyrinthine mind,
Roams through the corridors of thought to find
Inspiration hidden in whispered tones,
Amidst bustling streets and silent groves, alone.

They gaze upon the sky, the stars above,
And delve deep into the caverns of love.
In each fleeting moment, they seek to glean
The perfect words to make their verses keen.

With every stroke of pen, they strive to find
The elusive phrases, the thoughts enshrined.
Ten thousand times, they write and erase,
In search of lines that will embrace

The essence of their soul, their dreams untold,
As through sleepless nights and dawns they unfold.
In the journey of creation's flight,
They find the strength to bring their visions to light.

So let the poet wander, let them roam,
In search of words to turn their thoughts to home.
For in their quest, they find their art,
And share with the world their poet's heart.

In You, I Found What I Seek.

Amidst life's turbulence, you emerged, my ray of hope,
With you, I've found a steadiness, a place where storms subside.
In your embrace, I've known a peace profound,
A refuge from the battles we endure.

With you, I've found a love that knows no bound,
A bond so deep, so steady, so secure,
Grateful for your love in every form.

For every trial, every test we face,
You've been my rock, my shelter from the storm.
In you, I've found my home, my sacred space,
And in your love, I've found my strength, renewed.

Youth's Savored Love

Young hearts, naive, yearn,
Love's bittersweet embrace found,
Wisdom in the pain.

In the Words of Elders

Amidst whispers soft, wisdom resides,
A treasure trove where truth abides.
Though young and bright, some may ignore,
The wisdom shared from days of yore.

In tales spun by elders, secrets unfold,
Lessons learned, more precious than gold.
Yet fools disregard, in their haste,
The guidance offered, in wisdom laced.

Experience, a wine, aged with grace,
Savors of life, no time can erase.
But those who heed, with open mind,
Find richness in the truths they find.

Listen, oh youth, with open ears,
In their stories, wisdom appears.
Choose words wisely, listen with care,
To avoid life's pitfalls, if you dare.

So heed the counsel of the old and wise,
In their guidance, find the ultimate prize.
For in their tales, lies the key,
To unlock life's mysteries, and set our spirits
free.

Heroines Within: A Fairy Tale Manifesto

In the realm of dreams, where wishes take flight,
As a woman in a fairy tale, bathed in light.
With beauty like Snow White, a vision so rare,
And kindness like Cinderella, beyond compare.

Hair as radiant as Rubenzul's glow,
A symbol of strength, a majestic flow.
Smart and brave, like Bella from the East,
With a tender heart, where love finds its feast.

Embracing adventure, like Ariel's quest,
Exploring new realms, where hearts are blessed.
Sincere and pure, like Maleficent's gaze,
In the face of darkness, a guiding blaze.

With courage and compassion, like Anna's
embrace,
Breaking through barriers, with love and grace.
If you held all these qualities, where would you
stand?
In the midst of your story, hand in hand.

So let's celebrate the magic within,
In the fairy tale of life, where dreams begin.
With each virtue shining, bright and true,
Manifesting our best, in all that we do.

UNINVITED GUEST ON JUNE 29, 2024

Early morning on June twenty-nine,
Imphal Valley stirred with a fearful cry.
Voices echoing, the waters rising high,
An uninvited guest had arrived nearby.

Swiftly I rose to find the courtyard drowned,
Rushing waters, an unstoppable surge.
We hurried to gather what we could save,
As the flood engulfed, a relentless wave.

Plants drowned, animals lost and astray,
Lives shattered, swept in the flood's sway.
Boats ferrying those who had to leave,
Vehicles submerged, as waters heave.

Neighbours' dogs left in the dark,
At the dog park, waiting through the night,
confined.
Yearning for his mater, who couldn't return,
A loyal companion, in patience did he yearn.

Prayers whispered through the night,
Watching the waterline, ever so near.
Sleep eluded us, our mind full of fears,
Hoping the waters would not reach such a
height.

Each new day, we watched the waterline,
But only inches would slowly decline.
Our hopes hung on every small retreat,
As the flood's grip loosened in slow defeat.

Ten days the floodwaters ruled our land,
Leaving behind a landscaped, turned into a grey
ship.
Drinking water and supplies were sent by many
a hand,
Through agencies working to aid the land.

From the depths of despair, a strength we found,
In unity and courage, we stand our ground.
With each dawn, a chance to renew,
Rising from the flood, stronger and true.

The Youthful Skies

Beneath the canopy of youthful skies,
Where hearts entwine as dreams arise.
Easily we fall, vulnerable and true,
Through love's tempests, we navigate anew.

To taste love's essence a fleeting flame,
A gift of passion, where hearts reclaim.
For those who miss this sweet and salty taste,
Like skipping sugar's rush or salt's embrace,

Jealousy's dance, a wild, swirling tide,
Yet in its currents, we find our stride.
Life's journey unfolds, a winding trail,
Where dreams take flight, against the gale.

Focused on self, yet daring and free,
In this ode to youth, love's melody.
Let us embrace love's enchanting tune,
Swaying beneath the stars and moon.

For you, the vibrant youth, vivid and clear,
This poem paints your days with joy and fearless cheer.

The Feeling of Being Lost

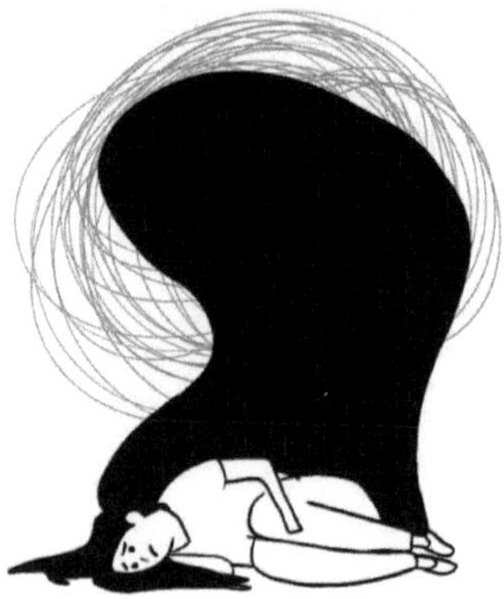

When nothing goes right and all seems astray,
I try to stay positive, though clouds block the
way.
Sometimes I envy my friends, their smiles so
bright,
While I struggle in darkness, yearning for light.

Some days I don't want to face the dawn,
To endure the struggles that stretch and yawn.
Silently, tears fall, doubts cloud my mind,
Wondering if the path I chose was unkind.

Emotions surge, sometimes I lose control,
And in frustration, I hurt those I hold.
Knowing I've caused pain, it burns inside,
Yet I can't calm myself, the pain I can't hide.

I believe this storm won't define my life,
There's a brighter path ahead, beyond the strife.
Someday, I'll be better, I'll find my way,
And I hope they'll forgive me as I grow each
day.

For life's journey is a winding, uncertain road,
With burdens to bear and truths to be told.
Through these struggles, I'll learn and grow,
From the darkest nights, new strengths will flow.

Seeking Within

Happiness is priceless,
A remedy for the soul.
Why do we search outside
When healing is within our control?
Richness beyond measure,
In tranquil moments found.
Why seek external wealth
When inner peace bounds?
Powerful in its presence,
Hope forever unbound?
What limits do we impose
When happiness knows no bounds?
Cheerful in every sunrise,
Mindful in every breath.
Why look elsewhere for joy
When each moment offers depth?
Strength in quiet resilience,

Contagious joy we share.
How does our inner strength
Inspire those around us to care?

Laughter echoing freely,
Grace in every stride.
What barriers dissolve
When happiness becomes our guide?
Compassion for the world,
Content in life's ride.
Can we find true peace
By embracing empathy wide?
Gratitude for each day,
Resilience through the storm,
How does gratitude transform
Every challenge into reform?
Freedom in our choices,
Empathy keeps us warm.
In what ways does empathy
Bring harmony and charm?
Kindness in every action,
Serenity in each night.
How does kindness shine
In the peaceful glow of twilight?
Optimism guiding paths,
Fulfilment shining bright.
What dreams do we pursue
With optimism's guiding light?
Love that knowns no bounds,

In every hue and view.
How does love, unconditional,
Enrich all that we pursue?
It resides within us,
True happiness, in all we do.
What discoveries await
When we seek happiness anew?

Fires of March

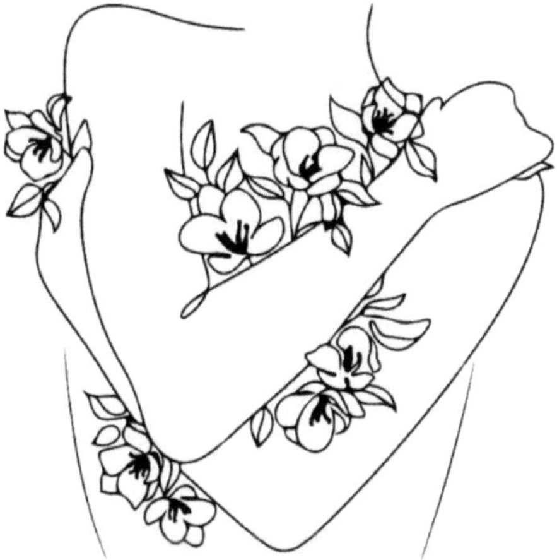

In March's bloom where Aries stands,
With fiery spirit, bold and grand.
In joy, their laughter fills the air,
A blaze of life beyond compare.

Through trials dark, they steadfast stand,
Facing challenges with steady hand.
Courage flows from deep within,
Their fearless hearts, they dare to win.

In love's embrace, their passion soars,
Romantic tales, they write in scores.
If heartache comes, they bear it strong,
With grace that lasts their whole life long.

Adventures bold, they seek the peak,
Where honour lies, and kindness speaks.
Each quest they take, they boldly chase,
Aries shines with boundless grace.

“Every Beauty Has a Bite”

Every rose that blooms in splendour bright,
Holds thorns that prick in the softest light.
Its petals soft, a fragrant dream,
Yet hidden barbs can make you scream.

The ocean’s waves, a lullaby,
Can crash and churn, can make you cry.
Its beauty vast, a sapphire spread,
Can pull you down to depths of dread.

A love that starts with passion's flame,
Can end in sorrow, heart's refrain.
The sweetest kiss, a gentle touch,
Can turn to wounds that hurt forever.

The mountain's peak, a sight to see,
Holds dangers where the climbers be.
Its heights inspire, a lofty goal,
Yet one misstep can take its toll.

The starry sky, a night's delight,
Can hide the void, the endless night.
Its twinkling lights, a cosmic show,
Yet shadows form where light won't go.

In every song that lifts the soul,
A mournful note can take its toll.
Its melody, a sweet embrace,
Can hide a tear on someone's face.

“Whisper of My Muse”

Why do I write poetry?
Not for one sole purpose,
But for myriad reasons.

I write when emotions overflow,
In sadness, when words fail to flow.
I write in joyous times,
To capture moments I cannot contain.

I write to explore imagination,
Crafting unique, innovative expression.
Words dance freely on the page,
Painting landscapes of my mind.

Poetry, a powerful medium,
communicates ideas, beliefs, perspectives,
Accepting me without judgment.
In its verses, I find solace,
A sanctuary for my soul’s voice.

It encourages introspection, guiding self-discovery,
Offering clarity, wisdom, insight.
Each line a journey inward,
Unveiling truths hidden within.

I write because I love it,
Connecting deeply with others,
Contributing to society's tapestry.
In every stanza, a connection blooms,
Threads of empathy binding hearts.

Fateful Encounter

Our paths crossed in our teenage years,
He recalls vividly the smile on my face,
As I carried the bamboo basket,
fetching water on my back,
Slowly, we became friends in the youthful haze.

Years drifted by, until fate's gentle hand,
Guided us to meet again on 24th night
December,
His flirtatious charm, m quiet delight,
He admired deeply the windows to my soul.

Time waltzed on, leading us down separate
lanes,
Yet destiny wove another unplanned meeting,
Amidst the bustling morning vegetable market,
I heard my name, turned to see him standing
grand.

Oh, how I wished I'd dressed a touch more refined,
As he stood by his car, a gentleman in black,
What if this is our last meeting? I should dress and look better,
These fleeting moments, regrets softly whisper.

When It Rains

Gentle drops caress the leaves,
A tender kiss from skies above,
In each droplet, the earth believes,
A gift of growth, a sign of love.

Roots drink deep, their thirst is quenched,
Green whispers rise, a soft refrain,
In every corner, life entrenched,
Plant lovers smile when it rains.

Bold and Innocent

A butterfly, with courage dressed,
In fields where dreams are lightly pressed.
Its wings, a canvas of dawn's soft light,
Chasing winds, embracing flight.

In every hue, a pure delight,
A heart unspoiled by worldly plight.
Through meadows fair, it dares to roam,
Gathering courage, finding home.

Oh, butterfly, both bold and true,
Teach us secrets, old and new.
In your gentle dance, we find our grace,
In whispered winds, a silent embrace.

The Quiet Truth of Love

True love is not the lighting strike,
Not thunder that shakes the skies,
It's more like rain that softly falls,
Gentle, steady, never tries.

It's not the blaze of burning fire,
That scorches all it meets,
But the warmth that lingers in the night,
When all the noise retreats.

It's not the grand, dynamic scene,
Where passion shouts its name,
But the look that speaks without a word,
The trust that stays the same.

True love’s a hand that holds your own,
When all the world feels lost,
A quiet bond that time can’t break,
No matter what the cost.

Hello

Hello, all things begin with a hello,
A word so simple, yet profound in its flow.
For some, it leads to dreams yet unseen,
For others, to paths where shadows convene.

A word so soft, yet laden with fate,
Hello can open or close the gate.
It brings both heaven and whispers of sorrow,
A duality life must borrow.

Is this the mystery borne on the breeze,
A hello that floats with such effortless ease?
Why greet the world if no path lies clear,
If steps are uncertain, and filled with fear?

We long for a hello that heals,
That brings us joy, where truth reveals,
Yet life, in wisdom, spins its thread,
Weaving hellos we sometimes dread.

Yet still, we utter it, hope in our hearts,
A hello that loves, and never departs.
In each hello, a promise does lie,
A journey begins, ‘neath the vast sky.

Are You Happy in This Modern World?

Are you happy in this world of haste,
Where moments slip by, too fleeting to taste?
Does your heart find rest in concrete veins,
Or drown in the rhythm of city rains?

In the age of screens and artificial glow,
Where real connection is rare and slow,
Do you feel whole in the endless scroll,
Or is there a void technology can't console?

We chase the new, the bright, the fast,
But do we forget the roots of the past?
Where the quiet of nature once held peace,
Now drowned by the hum of machine's release.

In a world of likes, where is the love?
In a sea of noise, what are we part of?
Are we fulfilled by the shine of it all,
Or does it only deepen the silent fall?

You walk through a maze of progress and steel,
But tell me, in truth, how does it feel?
Are you happy in this modern race,
Or longing for a simpler place?

When night falls and the city's asleep,
Do you dream of the life we sold so cheap?
Is there still a spark beneath the chase,
A deeper meaning in this modern space?

Unspoken Wish

In the quiet of the night,
Where shadows softly kiss,
A heart's silent flight,
An unspoken wish.

Glimmers in the starlit sky,
Dreams that never fade,
Hopes gently lie,
In moments we've made.

Beneath the moon's soft glow,
Whispers of a past,
Feelings seldom show,
Longings that will last.

In the silence, a plea,
A chance to truly be,
In the depth of night,
A wish takes flight.

Midnight Longing

In dreams, my past love gently shows,
Affection that still lingers and glows,
Yet you, who hold my heart so dear,
Rarely appear when night is near.

Why do they come, so real and true,
Leaving me sad when the night's through?
Come and fight for our love's embrace,
For I want nobody but you in this space.

I wish for you in dreams each night,
To share in love's soft, tender light.
Let us be close when darkness falls,
So I wake with your warmth, and feel your call.

The Path To Self-Respect

Without respect, I'll go,
When there's no trust, I'll leave,
With no value, I'll part ways,
If there is no care, I won't grieve.

When there's no love, I'll move on,
Without honour, I'll depart,
If there's no faith, I'll find my path,
When truth is lost, I'll guard my heart.

When no bond, I'll seek my peace,
Without warmth, I'll turn away,
In search of what my spirit needs,
I'll chase the light of a brighter day.

For self-respect, I make this stand,
To honour who I truly am,
I walk away from what's not true,
To find the strength to start anew.

The Silent Cry

Men hurt too, in silence they scream,
Crushed beneath society's gleam.
Labelled as providers, never allowed to fall,
They bear the weight, carrying it all.

In life, they shatter, hearts torn apart,
By expectations that tear at their heart.
Left broken by dreams they couldn't fulfil,
Choking on sorrow, but standing still.

Father crushed under demands so steep,
As they sacrifice dreams they can no longer keep.
Provider, protector, yet who protects them?
In this endless race, who counts their pain?

Brothers surrender what they cherish the most,
Sacrificing dreams, becoming ghosts.
They give, they serve, without a sound,
But who sees them when they break down?

Society commands, "Be strong, be bold,"
But inside they crumble, losing hold.
In a world that demands they never break,
Many are left drowning, for strength's sake.

Competition fierce, the stakes so high,
Some rise, but others silently die.
The pressure doesn't discriminate or spare,
It suffocates, leaves them gasping for air.

In their minds, storms rage and brew,
Struggling alone, with no one to turn to.
Some cannot bear the crushing strife,
And in their darkness, they end their life.

Society, hear this, understand,
Men are not stone, they are human, not grand.
They bleed, they break, they cry unseen,
They need our support, not just our dream.

Let them weep, let them fall,
It's time to dismantle this towering wall.
Acknowledge their pain, their silent cries,
For in their weakness, true strength lies.

No more should they suffer in silence,
Let their voices rise, let their pain be stirred.
It's time to listen, to break this chain,
Men hurt too, and they need to be seen.

The Edge of Kindness

Kindness is a beautiful thing,
But even beauty has its limits.
You give, you care, you pour yourself out,
Until one day, you feel empty.

You've always been the one to help.
The one to listen, the one to say yes,
But in the quiet moments,
When the world falls away,
You wonder: who's there for you?

It's not that you want to stop giving.
You just want to find where your kindness ends
And your own needs begin.

Because kindness isn't just about saying yes.
It's about knowing when to say no.
It's about drawing a line,
Not out of selfishness, but out of self-respect.

There's a strength in knowing your limits,
In understanding that you can't pour from an empty cup.
You have to fill yourself first—
With love, with peace, with boundaries.

So you learn to say no
Not because you care less,
But because you care enough—
About yourself and the people you love.

Kindness doesn't mean giving until
There's nothing left.
It means giving from a place of fullness
From a heart that's whole.

And that's the kind of kindness that lasts,
That truly makes a difference.

Beyond The Mirror's Glare

They'll say you're too thin, you need to eat,
Or too large, shrink down, admit defeat.
Too quick, slow down, take your time,
Too slow, hurry up, you're wasting mine.

Too loud, they say, you talk too much,
Or too silent, speak up, we need your touch.
Too bright, they warn, calm your fire,
Or too dull, where's your desire?

Judgement cast from every side,
Expectations impossible to abide.
But in this storm of endless critique,
It's your own voice you must seek.

For society's gaze is a fleeting thing,
A chorus of doubts that never sing.
In the silence beyond their cries,
You'll find the truth, the self that flies.

So rise above their fickle tune,
Embrace our rhythm, your own boon.
For in your heart, your soul, your grace,
Lies the strength to set your pace.

In The Smallest Ripples

Pay attention to the little things
If you seek clarity in your path.
In the ripple of a quiet stream,
Find the truth the world unveils.

Pay attention to the inner voice
If you yearn to know what you seek.
In the echoes of your soul's choice,
Find the guidance that you need.

Pay attention to his subtle gestures,
If you wish to see if he's right.
In the silent moments, small and tender,
Discover if his heart aligns with yours.

For in the minute, often overlooked,
Lie the answers you search for most.
In every detail, every glance,
Lies the map to love and understanding.

The Last Look

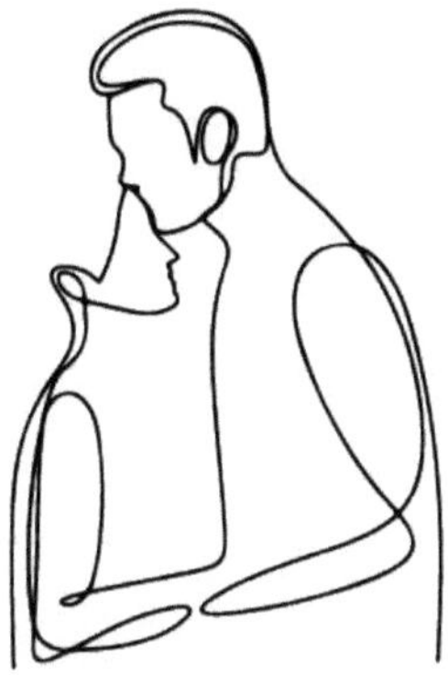

This is the last time,
The last time I'll see your face this close,
The last time our eyes will meet in this way,
The last time I'll trace every line, every curve,
The last time I'll memorize your features,
The last time I'll drink in your presence,
The last time I'll feel the warmth of your gaze,
The last time I'll hold this moment,
The last time I'll wish it would never end,
The last time…
The last time…
This is the last time,
And yet, I can't look away.

A Poet's Promise

If I am a star, I'd carve your name into the cosmos,
But I am not.
If I am a sea, I'd reveal my deepest treasures to you,
But I am not.
If I am a garden, I'd bloom the finest flowers for you,
But I am not.
If I am a millionaire, I'd take you to the ends of the earth,
But I'm not.
I am just a poet, with words to give,
Weaving love into each line, where our hearts truly live.
In the quiet solitude of ink and paper,
I sculpt a universe where our love grows ever greater.

Everybody Makes Mistakes

Everybody stumbles, everybody falls,
In this life, we're bound to heed the call,
Of errors made along the way,
But they don't shape us or make us stray.

A misstep here, a wrong turn there,
We carry burdens, but we can repair.
For mistakes don't define who we are,
They're lessons carved in every scar.

So hold your heart with tender grace,
Let go of the weight, forgive the past.
And when you falter again, as we all do,
Remember, it's the rising that defines you.

Slow Down

Slow down, my friend, the world will spin,
Rest your weary soul, let calm begin.
Sleep when you can, embrace the night,
For in old age, sleep may take flight.

Slow down, don't chase every fleeting tale,
Social media's lure can often pale.
What you see is just a mere disguise,
Don't let comparisons cloud your skies.

Slow down; when love slips through your hand,
What's not meant for you won't ever stand.
Accept the pain, let healing flow,
Don't lose yourself in sorrow's glow.

Slow down, this race, it has no end,
Chasing dreams that only bend.
You know yourself, you hold the key,
Don't shape your life to false decree.

Slow down, the thoughts can be snared,
One step at a time, with mindful care.
Your body, your heart, they're on your side,
Take it slow, and let peace abide.

The Weight They Carry

Quiet corners hold shadows that creep,
Divorce leaves echoes, cutting deep.
Children wear smiles, a fragile disguise,
While storms of sorrow brew in their eyes.

Shame wraps around them like chains of old,
Anxiety whispers, its grip ever bold.
Anger erupts like a volcano inside,
Sadness, a wave, they desperately hide.

Wishing for family, together and whole,
Longing for photos that capture their soul.
While others embrace in unbroken delight.
They dream of the day when everything's right.

Society watches with judgmental eyes,
Forgetting the truth that beneath the guise,
These little hearts bear a weight not their own,
Yet carry the burden as if they've grown.

Hope flickers dimly, a candle's soft glow,
In a world that feels cold, where few truly know.
Yet in their silence, a strength will rise,
For deep in their struggle, resilience lies.

Here's to the children, brave in their fight,
Navigating darkness, searching for light.
Their pain is not lost; it's a part of their song,
And through every struggle, they'll learn to be
strong.

When You Let Go Of Love

I held on tight to what we were,
A love that once felt so secure.
But in my grasp, it slowly frayed,
Like whispers lost in twilight's fade.

I clung to moments, to your face,
Hoping time would not erase
The laughter shared, the tender nights,
The promises in starlit lights.

But love, it cannot be confined,
Nor trapped in hearts, nor locked in mind.
To cage it is to watch it die,
A fading flame beneath the sky.

So I'll release you like the wind,
No need to fight what's destined to end.
I'll let you drift where you belong,
For in that space, love still stays strong.

In letting go, I've come to see,
Love doesn't fade, it sets you free.
And though apart, our hearts still know,
That sometimes love must let love go.

Wounds of Words

After the breakup, harsh words were thrown,
In the heat of pain, we cast our stones.

Each phrase a dagger, each shout a scar,
What once brought us joy now feels so far.

You were my comfort, my heart's gentle song,
Now those melodies feel so painfully wrong.

We traded affection for blame and despair,
Leaving shadows of anger hanging in the air.

But in the quiet, I still wonder why—
Were you the one, or was it a lie?

For though we spoke what we didn't mean,
The love we shared still lingers, unseen.

Now, in the silence, I question it all—
Was it love, or just the rise before the fall?

Beyond the Point

The day you said there's no point,
I found my purpose, clear and strong.

You asked me to walk away from you,
But staying felt where I belonged.

In your silence, I hear my truth,
A deeper voice that called me near.

Now I stand firm, unmoved by doubt,
For losing you brought me here.

Does True Love Exist?

Does true love exist, or is it but a dream,
A fleeting whisper in life's rushing stream?
Is it the touch that lingers when we part,
Or quiet comfort that soothes the heart?

Is it found in words, both soft and kind,
Or the silent moments where souls unwind?
Is it passion's fire, fiercely bright,
Or the steady glow that warms the night?

Perhaps true love is more than we see,
Not just the highs, or ecstasy.
It's in the giving, the patient stay,
The tender mending when hearts betray.

True love, if real, is never pure,
It's flawed and raw, yet still endures.
It's found in two hearts, though scarred and worn,
Choosing each other in the storm.

Yes, true love exists, though hard to find,
A rare sweet bond that's soul-aligned.
It's not in grand gestures or fleeting bliss,
But in the truth of an honest kiss.

A Fool's Choice

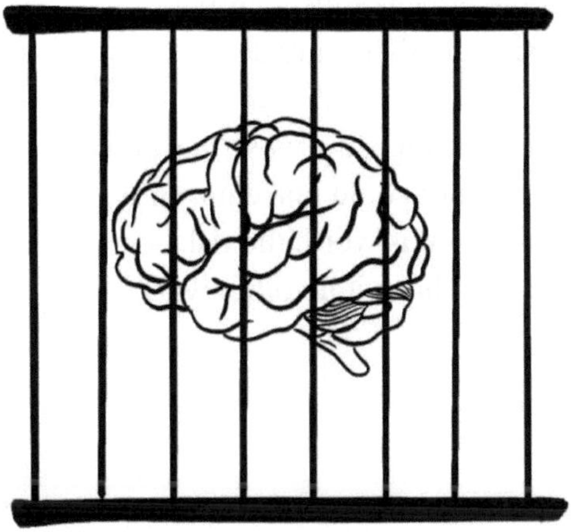

If loving you makes me the fool,
Then let me wear that name with pride,
For I won't trade your tender touch
For wisdom's hollow, empty stride.

If love's a game with dangerous stakes,
Then let me play, and risk it all,
I'd rather face regret unknown
Than never feel your heart's sweet call.

For in my soul, I'm sure of this—
You are the one, my perfect fate,
And though the world may doubt or scorn,
I choose you, never to hesitate.

You'll never let me fall alone,
I trust in you with every breath,
And if the price is folly's crown,
I'll wear it gladly till my death.

Again and again, I'd choose this path,
No wiser word could make me stray,
For loving you is worth the risk—
And I would have it no other way.

My First Kiss

It was a winter night, cold and still,
You reached for my hand, bending my will,
With a pull, drawing me closer, lost under
moonlit skies.
My heart raced, caught between thrill and fear.

Your touch, so gentle, yet firm on my skin,
Calming the storm that trembled within.
Your hands slid to my shoulders, melting the
cold,
In that moment, your love made me bold.

A soft gaze lingered, warmth in your eyes,
As your lips sought mine in a soft, slow trace.
Time stood still as our hearts entwined,
In that kiss, our souls were perfectly aligned.

The world disappeared in that fleeting touch,
Heaven seemed real, but oh, never too much.
In my teenage years, that sacred bliss,
I still remember—my very first kiss.

There Are Times

There are times you wanna say "I love you"
But you cannot,
Words heavy in your heart,
A silence you cannot break.

There are times you wanna say "I miss you"
But you cannot,
Your voice trapped in your chest,
Longing to be heard.

There are times you wanna say "Don't worry,
everything will be alright"
But you cannot,
Your comfort trapped behind walls,
Emotions left unstirred.

There are times you wanna know how they are,
But you cannot,
The distance a cruel barrier,
Your concern left unsent.

There are times you wanna call and hear their voice,
But you cannot,
The phone a silent witness
To the love that you meant.

Time plays a wonderful game.
Sometimes it gives you all you want,
Moment of pure happiness, joy that feels so near.
But sometimes time takes everything you have, leaving you hopeless,
A thief in the night, stripping away all that you hold dear.

Āmā: The Unseen Hero

In the quiet corners of our town, a legend unfolds,
A single mother, whose strength is a story untold.
She runs a small grocery, where every need finds its place,
More than just shelved goods, it's a testament to grace.

Known to all as Āmā, a name cherished and dear,
More than just "mother", it's a symbol of all she endures here.

Her life, a rich tapestry of struggles and strife,
Yet each customer greeted with laughter's light,
Her joy, a beacon, her spirit ever bright.

In the stillness of night, when the world softly sleeps,
She whispers prayers for her children, her love runs deep.
She taught us resilience in a world so cold,
To face each challenge with courage, both brave and bold.
Her laughter rings out, defying the silent night,
Against a world that often demands her quiet might.
With every smile, she masks the weight she bears,
Her burdens heavy, yet she lovingly shares.

Her life a dance of sorrow and hope intertwined,
With private tears shed, but her faith remains aligned.
In her quiet room, she communes with the Divine,
Seeking strength and solace in her sacred shrine.
She carries her siblings close, with a tender and true,
And tends to her aging parents, their strength subdued.
Her love, a river flowing endlessly,

Nurturing those around her, in boundless
empathy.

Āmā, the unsung hero, her story remains veiled,
A warrior in the mundane, with a heart that
never failed.
Through hardships and trials, she stands ever
tall,
A beacon of resilience, a heroine to us all.
My mother, my superhero, in life's gentle
scenes,
A true testament to love, faith, and grace, she
redeems.

The Paradox of Happiness

Who said money can't bring joy to life?
For without it, I struggle, amidst the strife.
A world of desires, dreams, and need,
Money is the soil where ambitions seed.

Without its comfort, I find myself cold,
Dreams of warmth, yet it's hard to hold.
They say happiness is free, it's just a state,
But how can one smile with an empty plate?

Money may not buy love, or true peace,
But it grants a moment's sweet release.
A roof above, a meal to share,
In its absence, life feels unfair.

It’s not the gold, nor the lavish things,
But the simple peace of what it brings.
Security, health, a chance to thrive,
Without these, it’s hard to feel alive.

So, who said money can’t make me glad?
For without it, how can I not be sad?
In a world where it’s needed, how can I cope,
Without it, happiness feels like a distant hope.

But amidst this chase, let’s not forget,
True wealth lies in the moment we collect,
Yet, with money, those moments seem near,
A balance of joy, without fear.

So, who said money can’t make me happy?
It’s not about greed, but living stress-free.
In this paradox of life we tread,
Happiness and money, both tightly wed.

The Shared Crown

A crown worn alone may gleam bright,
But its luster fades in the solitude of night.
For what is a queen, if she does not see,
The strength in the bonds of solidarity?

A true queen rises, not by the fall of others,
But by lifting her sisters, her friends, her
mothers.
She knows that to shine in a lasting way,
She must give her light, not take it away.

Each woman is a thread in a grand design,
A pattern of resilience, a lifeline intertwined.
Alone, we are strong, but together we blaze,
A fire that illuminates the darkest of days.

The world is wide, but smaller still,
When we stand as one, with an unbreakable will.
For in unity lies our deepest might,
To build, to heal, to bring forth light.

So let us share this crown of gold,
In hands that uplift, in stories untold.
For a kingdom of one is not a kingdom at all,
But a collective spirit that refuses to fall.

We are queens, not by our singular reign,
But by the support we give, the love we sustain.
And when we rise, we do so together,
Creating a world that is brighter, forever.

This is the crown we all can bear,
A legacy of strength, a promise to care.
For in the unity of women, there lies the key,
To a future of hope, where all are free.

Unbound

When you let the whispers of quarrels fade,
And burdens of fleeting moments slip,
You rise like the calm of a brewing storm,
With a future as bright as the stars' cool grip.

The world opens wide when you turn within,
Seeking the truth that your heart believes,
They may carve their paths in borrowed dreams,
But your soul is meant to walk with ease.

Society speaks with a thousand chains,
Pressing you into shapes unknown,
But why should your fire bow to their winds,
When you were born to stand out loud?

Let their shadows dissolve in your wake,
For your light is meant to carve the skies.
In the quiet of self, you'll find the truth—
A world beyond their thin disguise.

Rise from the ashes of their desires,
Untamed, unbroken, in every breath.
The world would yield to your silent flame,
When you walk in your light each day.

Be not what they wish, but what you are—
A force too wild to ever confine.
And in the mirror of your soul's embrace,
You'll see the stars and the earth align.

Fall Out of Love

How could you be so cruel,
I can't fathom who you've become.
I fell for your sweet, honeyed words,
Now tremble, left cold and numb.

I gave my all, my heart, my soul,
Yet now I'm lost, a shattered whole.
Did you love me once, was it ever true,
Or were you just playing a part, slipping through?

You taught me how to fall, how to care,
Now teach me how to bear this despair,
For "moving on" is easy to say,
But harder to live with day by day.

Show me how you can behave this way,
As if we meant nothing at all.
Love was sweet, but its end was cruel,
And now I'm drowning, wondering if you still care.

Teach me how to fall out of love,
For I can't push these memories above.
They linger, they haunt, they won't let go,
Whispering your name in an endless echo.

Goodbye

When saying goodbye brings a tear,
It shows we've shared a bond so pure,
Each laugh, each whisper, cherished here,
A love that time cannot obscure.

The moments we've spent side by side,
Will linger on through all our days,
Your touch, your smile, like summer's tide,
In our hearts, these memories blaze.

These tears that fell, so soft and kind,
Reveal how deep our love has grown,
A bittersweet and tender sign,
Of how our hearts have truly known.

So let these tears flow, gentle and free,
For they honour what we've shared,
Goodbye is but a brief decree,
We'll meet again, and joy be declared.

Daddy

Daddy, I see the silver strands,
But your hands still work with love and care.
You rise early each day to toil and strive
To make sure joy fills the air.

I saw your tears when strength gave way,
When the burden felt too much to bear.
And I heard your wish for a brother's hand,
To stand beside you, face life's snare.

Alone you fight against the tide,
Amongst stronger kin, you stand your ground.
But don't you worry, Daddy dear,
In our hearts, your efforts resound.

The world may ask so much from you,
Say what they will, demand and pry—
But we know how much you've tried,
And in your love, we testify.

Your dress with grace, your fashion speaks,
A man of strength, both calm and neat.
But most of all, it’s who you are—
Our loving Daddy, pure at heart.

Wings of Wax

You fly so high with wings of wax,
Believing you've mastered every sky,
Above the clouds, no fear of cracks,
You think no storm could make you cry.

The sun, a friend, you mock its heat,
As if its fire cannot touch your pride,
But when it melts beneath your feet,
You'll tumble down with nowhere to hide.

The ground will greet your foolish fall,
With whispered truths in every stone,
Life's quiet hand will catch it all,
And remind you, you're not alone.

For wings of wax will always melt,
In the blaze of unearned might,
So tread with care, and humbly belt,
For life will humble even the height.

If You Don't Try, You Will Never Know

In shadow of doubt, dreams quietly rest,
A heart full of wishes, too scared to test.

What if the mountain you fear to ascend
Hold treasures of courage waiting to blend?

Each moment you linger, a chance slips away,
For life's sweetest truths bloom in the fray.

So dare to take risks, let your spirit ignite,
Embrace the unknown, let your passions flow.

The journey may challenge, the path may be steep,
But the dreams left unchased are the ones that we keep.

With each step you take, new horizons will show,
For if you don't try, you will never know.

Echoes of a Forgotten Queen

She once danced in the whispers of the crowd,
A name on every tongue, her grace avowed.
In the garden of life, she bloomed so bright,
A beauty so rare, it captured the light.
Her dreams were vast, her will like fire,
Surrounded by those who could only admire.
She walked with pride, head held high,
Believing forever she'd rule in fame.

But the world is a battlefield, cruel and sly,
Where even the brightest stars can lose their sky.
She slipped from the heights, unnoticed at first,
Lost in a race, in a world so cursed.

Now she stumbles in shadows, gasping for air,
A queen dethroned, on the edge of death.
Her heart cries out in silent despair,
Seeking redemption in a world so unfair.

With hands clasped tight, she whispers a plea,
To the heavenly Father, she bends her knee.
"Forgive me, Father, for where I've strayed,
If there's still a spark deep within, let it not fade.

Let it shine again, through darkness and pain,
Guide me back to the path I once claimed.
For in this world, I seek not the throne,
But the strength to rise, to find my own.

Let me rise from the ashes of defeat,
A queen reborn, in grace complete."

Pukreila/Phukreila, The Peace Maker

In Tangkhul hills, where old ways lie,
Not just one, but many stood high—
Bridging villages, hands entwined,
Leaving roots and kin behind.

Known as Pukreila/Phukreila, fierce and wise,
With courage bright in steady eyes,
Daughters of one land, wives of another,
Bound by love, yet kin to all others.

In days of war and shadowed skies,
When head-hunters roamed with watchful eyes,
They bore the peace no blade could break,
Silent strength for their people's sake.

To harm them breached all sacred trust,
For Pukreila's place was fair and just.
In Tangkhul hills, their spirit deep,
An ancestral vow we strive to keep.

Lazy Day Delight

Today's a day for staying in,
Where wining means I'll sleepily grin.
No rush to move, no grand success—
Just me, my couch, my comfiest sweats.

The world spins on, but I stay still,
Watching clouds as time stands still.
I've mastered snacks and naps galore,
A lazy art some just ignore.

So here I lay, without a care,
Messy bun and tangled hair.
For on this day, I'm happily free—
The world can wait; it's time for me!

Phases of Longing

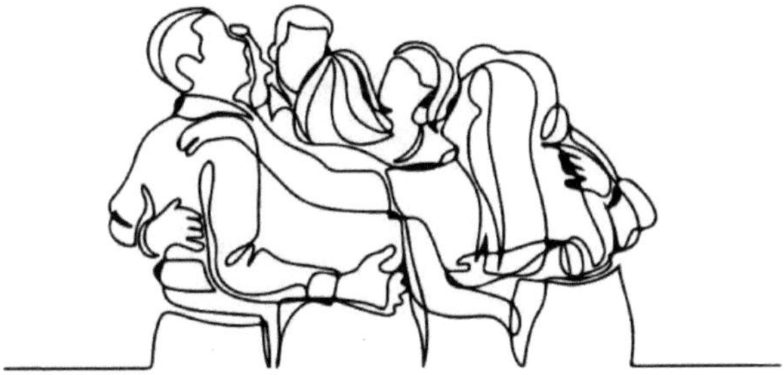

In high school hall, I watched them soar,
Those college kids, who opened doors,
With dreams ablaze and futures wide,
I envied their freedom, their carefree stride.

Then college came, and I joined the fray,
Yet found myself wishing for a different play—
The working souls, with purpose and gain,
Living lives where time felt less like a chain.
Now here I linger, caught in the blend,
Yearning for moments that never quite end.
High school's laughter, college's quest,
Each stage a chapter, each phase a test.

Oh, how I wish to rewind the reel,
To relish the joy, the trill, the feel.
Yet in this longing, a truth I see:
Each fleeting phase shaped the heart of me.

Unyielding Worth

I don't care what the world has to say,
Their judgments won't dim my fierce, fiery way.
This life is my canvas; I'll paint it on my own,
Unapologetic, I'll stand on my own.

If love isn't shown, I won't shed a tear,
I rise like a phoenix, strong without fear.
I know my worth; it's a flame deep inside,
A force unquenchable, a powerful tide.

So bring on the doubters; I'll stand tall and
proud,
With my head held high, I'll defy every crowd.
For I am a warrior, unbreakable free—
Knowing my worth, I'll shape my own destiny.

The Paradox of Goodbye

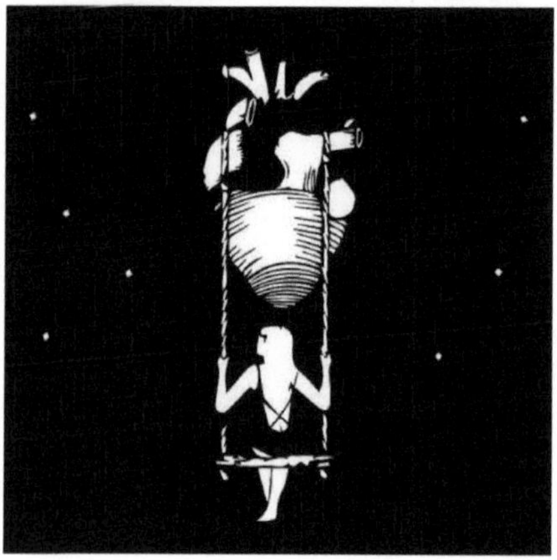

Why is goodbye a goodbye, when it isn't truly so?
Why does it always carry a hint of sorrow, subtle yet slow?

A goodbye draped in shadows, yet bathed in a gentle light,
A whisper of longing in the hush of the night,

Is it the finality, the end of a chapter's page,
Or the silent promise of meeting after an age?

Goodbye, a paradox, a blend of joy and pain,
A fleeting farewell with hopes to meet again.

For every goodbye carries a hidden plea,
A wish for another hello, another memory.

So, goodbye is never truly the end,
But a quiet promise that our paths will again
bend.

A Wish For Softness

I've heard enough of strength and survival's
creed.
Of battles to face and resilience to breed.
Why must we strive like heroes so bold,
With armour and shields and hearts turned cold?

Would it be wrong to wish for a world
Where softness unfurls, with dreams uncurled?
A place where I walk unguarded, unbound,
Where love flows freely, like light all around.

I long for the joy of a child's pure play,
Where trust comes easy, with no price to pay.
A world without shadows of envy or spite,
Just laughter and warmth, hearts open and
bright.

I crave a haven, gentle and calm,
Where no armour's needed, just love as my balm.
Where I don't need strength to face each day,
But find peace in the softness, where kindness stays.

So here's my wish, a prayer, a plea—
For a world that's gentle, where souls roam free.
Where I leave behind the battles and fears,
And live in a softness that's pure and clear.

The Measure of You

How great you are, in a world that sings your name,
How beautiful you are, yet beauty fades the same.
How powerful you are, a force that none dare bind,
How successful you are, with the world beneath your mind.

How rich you are, in treasures others seek,
How intelligent you are, with knowledge deep and sleek.
How brave you are, in storms you do not flee,
How magnificent you are, as grand as one can be.

But know this truth, no crown can hide,
Without kindness, your spirit's hollow inside.
For what are you, if love you can't bestow?
A hollow echo, proud yet bare.

Let your power and wealth lift those who fall,
For in kindness and humanity lies the mightiest call.
The world remembers not riches or fame,
But hearts that loved, untouched by shame.

Whispers to my Teenage self

Oh, restless heart, so eager to soar,
In the mirror's gaze, don't seek for more.
Each change that trembles beneath your skin,
Is a chance to discover the strength within.

Cherish your friends, those souls by your side,
In laughter and tears, let your hearts collide.
They'll weather the storms and dance in the rain,
For in shared memories, love's never in vain.

Don't chase perfection; it's a fleeting ghost,
In flaws and in scars, you'll find what matters most.
Each stumble, each tear, is a thread in your tale,
A testament of courage, a journey unveiled.

When the weight of the world feels heavy and tight,
Breathe deep, hold your heart, and let in the light.
For it's okay to falter, to feel lost or alone,
In those fragile moments, your spirit has grown.

Dare to dream wildly, let your passions ignite,
Your voice is a beacon, your truth is your light.
So forge your own path, let your heart lead the way,
For you're not just a teen; you're a world on display.

Embrace this sweet chaos, each joy and each pain,
In the tapestry woven, both sunshine and rain.
For this season of youth is a gift to unfold,
A story of courage, of beauty, of bold.

9 789360 943226

Printed by Libri Plureos GmbH in Hamburg, Germany